THE TRUTH ABOUT

THE
TRIBULATION

D1609660

THOMAS ICE AND
TIMOTHY DEMY

HARVEST HOUSE PUBLISHERS
Eugene, Oregon 97402

Pocket Prophecy Series

The Truth About 2000 A.D. and
Predicting Christ's Return

The Truth About Jerusalem
in Bible Prophecy

The Truth About the Antichrist
and His Kingdom

The Truth About the Last Days' Temple

The Truth About the Millennium

The Truth About the Rapture

THE TRUTH ABOUT THE TRIBULATION

Copyright © 1996 by Pre-Trib Research Center
Published by Harvest House Publishers
Eugene, Oregon 97402

ISBN 1-56507-406-8

Printed in the United States of America.

97 98 99 00 01 02 / BF / 9 8 7 6 5 4 3

Contents

About this series...

The Pocket Prophecy series is designed to provide readers with a brief summary of individual topics and issues in Bible prophecy. For quick reference and ease in studying, the works are written in a question-and-answer format. The questions follow a logical progression so that people who read straight through will receive a greater appreciation for the topic and the issues involved. The volumes are thorough, though not exhaustive, and can be used as a set or as single-volume studies. Each issue is fully documented and contains a bibliography of recommended reading for those people who desire to pursue their study in greater depth.

The theological perspective presented throughout the series is that of premillennialism and pretribulationism. The authors recognize that this is not the only position embraced by evangelical Christians, but we believe that it is the most widely held and prominent perspective. It is also our conviction that premillennialism and, specifically, pretribulationism, best explains the prophetic plan of God as revealed in the Bible.

The study of prophecy and its puzzling pieces is an endeavor which is detailed and complex—but not beyond comprehension or resolution. It is open to error, misinterpretation, and confusion. Such possibilities should not, however, cause any Christian to shy away from either the study of prophecy or engagement in honest and helpful discussions about it. The goal of this series is to provide all those who desire to better understand the Scriptures with a concise and consistent tool. If you will do the digging, the rewards will be great and the satisfaction will remain with you as you grow in your knowledge and love of our Lord Jesus Christ and His Word.

INTRODUCTION

Almost everyone has experienced turbulent and traumatic times during which there was great uncertainty or perhaps even enormous pain and sorrow. Such times are often periods of individual, familial, and perhaps even national crisis in which every personal, physical, and emotional resource is called into action in order to successfully endure the problem. Sorrow, grief, persecution, tragedy, catastrophe, famine, war, and uncertainty are all very real dynamics in daily life and newspaper headlines. However, according to the Bible, there will be a future time of even greater agony known as "the tribulation." This era will come after the rapture of the church and will be the greatest period of suffering the world has known. It will be the ultimate "future shock."

Wall Street's economic forecasters and speculators are often divided into optimists and pessimists (or "bulls" and "bears") based upon their "reading" of economic indicators and trends. In this same sense, interpreters of the Bible can read its prophetic passages and understand much of God's plan for the future. The difference with prophecy is that through careful and prayerful study, much of the speculation can be removed. Unlike tomorrow's markets, God's plan is clear and certain. Does belief in the rapture necessitate that Christians be pessimistic and apathetic? Certainly not! We are to be realistic and expectant. We are realistic about the future and we are expectant about the coming of the Lord Jesus Christ for His church. However, we also acknowledge that once the rapture occurs there will be a time of intense worldwide tribulation.

The Bible has more to say about these seven years than about any other prophetic time period. During these seven years, the Antichrist will emerge, persecution of new Christians and the Jewish people will ensue, and the great battle of Armageddon and the second coming of Christ will transpire.

The New Testament teaches that the current church age will also include trials and tribulation. Jesus said, "In the world you have tribulation, but take courage; I have overcome the world" (John 16:33). The apostle Paul warned, "And indeed, all who desire to live godly in Christ Jesus will be persecuted" (2 Timothy 3:12). However, the world's persecution of the church in this age is not the wrath of God. The future tribulation will be a time of God's wrath upon a Christ-rejecting world—a time from which the church has been promised by our Lord to be exempted (Revelation 3:10; 1 Thessalonians 1:10; 5:9).

Christians can daily live in confidence that human history will end with Jesus Christ as the Victor. The future is certain. Yet Jesus told His disciples that before the final victory, "There will be a great tribulation, such as has not occurred since the beginning of the world until now, nor ever will" (Matthew 24:21). In its intensity and agony, it will be unfortunate and undesirable. But its certainty and course is not unforeseen or unpredicted. The Bible says that it will be tragic but true.

P A R T   1

What Is the Tribulation?

1. Where does the Bible teach about the tribulation?

Old Testament Passages

Throughout the Bible there are many direct and indirect references to the tribulation.[1] One of the first and earliest Old Testament passages to prophesy of this period is found in Deuteronomy 4:27-31. These verses foretell both the scattering of the Jews and their restoration with the Lord if they seek Him:

> And the LORD will scatter you among the peoples, and you shall be left few in number among the nations, where the LORD shall drive you. And there you will serve gods, the work of man's hands, wood and stone, which neither see nor hear nor eat nor smell. But from there you will seek the LORD your God, and you will find Him if you search for Him with all your heart and

all your soul. When you are in distress and all these things have come upon you, in the latter days, you will return to the LORD your God and listen to His voice. For the LORD your God is a compassionate God; He will not fail you nor destroy you nor forget the covenant with your fathers which He swore to them.

Before Israel had set foot in their promised land, the Lord foretold an outline of their entire history (included in the book of Deuteronomy). Their destiny is said to be a time of "distress" or "tribulation" (KJV) "in the latter days" right before Israel "will return to the LORD your God and listen to His voice." Later in Deuteronomy, Moses expands upon this time of tribulation and notes that its purpose will include a time of retribution to the Gentiles for their ill treatment of the Jews. Note Deuteronomy 30:7:

And the LORD your God will inflict all these curses [Deuteronomy 28] on your enemies and on those who hate you, who persecuted you.

Continuing along the same line, Isaiah 26:20,21 notes that the tribulation includes the purpose of punishing the inhabitants of the earth for their sin. This passage also labels the tribulation an "indignation" from which Israel was to hide herself:

Come, my people, enter into your rooms, and close your doors behind you; hide for a little while, until indignation runs its course. For behold, the LORD is about to come out from His place to punish the inhabitants of the earth for their iniquity; and the earth will reveal her bloodshed, and will no longer cover her slain.

Isaiah continues to describe the Lord's wrath and judgment of the tribulation on behalf of Israel in Isaiah 34:2,3,8:

For the LORD's indignation is against all the nations, and His wrath against all their armies; He has utterly destroyed them, He has given them over to slaughter. So their slain will be thrown out, and their corpses will give off their stench, and the mountains will be drenched with their blood.... For the LORD has a day of vengeance, a year of recompense for the cause of Zion.

In the preaching of Jeremiah there is also reference to the tribulation. Not only did Jeremiah predict the Babylonian captivity of the Jews, but he also foretold of a time of yet-future trials for Israel. We read of this time in Jeremiah 30:5-9, which is often known as "the time of Jacob's trouble":

> For thus says the LORD, "I have heard a sound of terror, of dread, and there is no peace. Ask now, and see, if a male can give birth. Why do I see every man with his hands on his loins, as a woman in childbirth? And why have all faces turned pale? Alas! for that day is great, there is none like it; and it is the time of Jacob's distress, but he will be saved from it. And it shall come about on that day," declares the LORD of hosts, "that I will break his yoke from off their neck, and will tear off their bonds; and strangers shall no longer make them their slaves. But they shall serve the LORD their God, and David their king, whom I will raise up for them."

One of the most important passages for the study of the future is Daniel 9:24-27:

> Seventy weeks have been decreed for your people and your holy city, to finish the transgression, to make an end of sin, to make atonement for iniquity, to bring in everlasting righteousness, to seal up vision and prophecy, and to anoint the most holy place. So you are to know and discern that from the issuing of a decree to restore and rebuild Jerusalem until Messiah the Prince there will be seven weeks and sixty-two weeks; it will be built again, with plaza and moat, even in times of distress. Then after the sixty-two weeks the Messiah will be cut off and have nothing, and the people of the prince who is to come will destroy the city and the sanctuary. And its end will come with a flood; even to the end there will be war; desolations are determined. And he will make a firm covenant with the many for one week, but in the middle of the week he will put a stop to sacrifice and grain offering; and on the wing of abominations will come one who makes desolate, even until a complete destruction, one that is decreed, is poured out on the one who makes desolate.

In these four verses Daniel provides a clear and concise framework for prophetic study. This is a critical passage. A proper understanding of these verses provides students of prophecy with Scriptural signposts. From this passage we learn that the tribulation is a seven-year period, divided by the "abomination of desolation" into two three-and-a-half-year periods. Since Daniel's 70 weeks are 70 weeks of years, the final week of years (i.e., the tribulation) would thus be a seven-year period. Note the diagram on page 18 for further details and explanations.

Like Jeremiah, Daniel calls this future period "a time of distress." In Daniel 12:1 this time is described not just as "a time of distress," but also as a time when Israel "will be rescued":

> Now at that time Michael, the great prince who stands guard over the sons of your people, will arise. And there will be a time of distress such as never occurred since there was a nation until that time; and at that time your people, everyone who is found written in the book, will be rescued.

The whole book of Joel is about "the day of the Lord," which is a synonym for "the tribulation." Notice a couple of citations from Joel which refer to the tribulation:

> Alas for the day! For the day of the LORD is near, and it will come as destruction from the Almighty (1:15).

> Blow a trumpet in Zion, and sound an alarm on My holy mountain! Let all the inhabitants of the land tremble, for the day of the LORD is coming; surely it is near, a day of darkness and gloom, a day of clouds and thick darkness. As the dawn is spread over the mountains, so there is a great and mighty people; there has never been anything like it, nor will there be again after it to the years of many generations (2:1,2).

The prophet Amos, a shepherd from the Judean town of Tekoa, also prophesied about the tribulation in Amos 5:18-20:

> Alas, you who are longing for the day of the LORD, for what purpose will the day of the LORD be to you? It will

be darkness and not light; as when a man flees from a
lion, and a bear meets him, or goes home, leans his hand
against the wall, and a snake bites him. Will not the day
of the LORD be darkness instead of light, even gloom
with no brightness in it?

Even though Zephaniah is one of the smallest books in the
Bible, one of the most important passages relating to the tribulation is found there. The Lord, through Zephaniah, just about
exhausts the thesaurus as He pours out a vivid description of the
tribulation in Zephaniah 1:14-18:

Near is the great day of the LORD, near and coming very
quickly; listen, the day of the LORD! In it the warrior
cries out bitterly. A day of wrath is that day, a day of
trouble and distress, a day of destruction and desolation,
a day of darkness and gloom, a day of clouds and thick
darkness, a day of trumpet and battle cry, against the
fortified cities and the high corner towers. And I will
bring distress on men, so that they will walk like the
blind, because they have sinned against the LORD; and
their blood will be poured out like dust, and their flesh
like dung. Neither their silver nor their gold will be able
to deliver them on the day of the LORD's wrath; and all
the earth will be devoured in the fire of His jealousy, for
He will make a complete end, indeed a terrifying one, of
all the inhabitants of the earth.

Other Old Testament prophecies of this era include Joel
2:28-32 and Isaiah 2:12-22; 24 (this is not an exhaustive list).

New Testament Passages

The New Testament, building upon an Old Testament foun-
dation, expands our picture of the tribulation. The first extended
passage to deal with the tribulation in the New Testament is
Matthew 24:4-28 (see also Mark 13; Luke 17:22-37; and Luke
21:5-36 for parallel passages). In this discourse, Jesus describes
for the disciples the tribulation period. In verses 4-14, He speaks
about the first half of the tribulation, and in verses 15-28, He
describes the second half leading up to the second coming.
According to Jesus, the tribulation will be intense and extensive

and will include both human and natural disasters. Of the first three and a half years He says:

> See to it that no one misleads you. For many will come in My name, saying, "I am the Christ," and will mislead many. And you will be hearing of wars and rumors of wars; see that you are not frightened, for those things must take place, but that is not yet the end. For nation will rise against nation, and kingdom against kingdom, and in various places there will be famines and earthquakes. But all these things are merely the beginning of birth pangs. Then they will deliver you to tribulation, and will kill you, and you will be hated by all nations on account of My name. And at that time many will fall away and will deliver up one another and hate one another. And many false prophets will arise, and will mislead many. And because lawlessness is increased, most people's love will grow cold. But the one who endures to the end, he shall be saved. And this gospel of the kingdom shall be preached in the whole world for a witness to all the nations, and then the end shall come (Matthew 24:4-14).

Jesus then told the disciples that the second half of the tribulation would be no better than the first half. In fact, the trauma and suffering would escalate to such a point that it would end only after the battle of Armageddon and the second coming of Christ:

> Therefore when you see the ABOMINATION OF DESOLATION which was spoken of through Daniel the prophet, standing in the holy place (let the reader understand), then let those who are in Judea flee to the mountains; let him who is on the housetop not go down to get the things out that are in his house; and let him who is in the field not turn back to get his cloak. But woe to those who are with child and to those who nurse babes in those days! But pray that your flight may not be in the winter, or on a Sabbath; for then there will be a great tribulation, such as has not occurred since the beginning of the world until now, nor ever shall. And unless those days had been cut short, no life would have been saved; but for the sake of the elect those days shall be cut short. Then if

anyone says to you, "Behold, here is the Christ," or "There He is," do not believe him. For false Christs and false prophets will arise and will show great signs and wonders, so as to mislead, if possible, even the elect. Behold, I have told you in advance. If therefore they say to you, "Behold, He is in the wilderness," do not go forth, or, "Behold, He is in the inner rooms," do not believe them. For just as the lightning comes from the east, and flashes even to the west, so shall the coming of the Son of Man be. Wherever the corpse is, there the vultures will gather.

Paul's Thessalonian epistles have been characterized as the Pauline Apocalypse, since they deal extensively with the prophetic. Twice—in 1 Thessalonians 1:10 and 5:9—Paul refers to the tribulation when speaking of a future time of wrath (see also Romans 5:9):

> . . . and to wait for His Son from heaven, whom He raised from the dead, that is Jesus, who delivers us from the wrath to come.

> For God has not destined us for wrath, but for obtaining salvation through our Lord Jesus Christ.

In 2 Thessalonians 2:1,2, Paul tells his readers that they should not be deceived into thinking that the tribulation (i.e., the day of the Lord) had already started:

> Now we request you, brethren, with regard to the coming of our Lord Jesus Christ, and our gathering together to Him, that you may not be quickly shaken from your composure or be disturbed either by a spirit or a message or a letter as if from us, to the effect that the day of the Lord has come.

He then continues in verses 3-13 to further describe some of the events of the tribulation era:

> Let no one in any way deceive you, for it will not come unless the apostasy comes first, and the man of lawlessness is revealed, the son of destruction, who opposes and exalts himself above every so-called god or object

of worship, so that he takes his seat in the temple of God, displaying himself as being God. Do you not remember that while I was still with you, I was telling you these things? And you know what restrains him now, so that in his time he may be revealed. For the mystery of lawlessness is already at work; only he who now restrains will do so until he is taken out of the way. And then that lawless one will be revealed whom the Lord will slay with the breath of His mouth and bring to an end by the appearance of His coming; that is, the one whose coming is in accord with the activity of Satan, with all power and signs and false wonders, and with all the deception of wickedness for those who perish, because they did not receive the love of the truth so as to be saved. And for this reason God will send upon them a deluding influence so that they might believe what is false, in order that they all may be judged who did not believe the truth, but took pleasure in wickedness. But we should always give thanks to God for you, brethren beloved by the Lord, because God has chosen you from the beginning for salvation through sanctification by the Spirit and faith in the truth.

The most extensive biblical comments on the tribulation are found in the writings of John, specifically in Revelation 6–19. In these chapters, John provides a detailed exposition of the tribulation days. An example of John's specific mention of the tribulation can be seen in Revelation 7:14:

> And I said to him, "My lord, you know." And he said to me, "These are the ones who come out of the great tribulation, and they have washed their robes and made them white in the blood of the Lamb."

These chapters in Revelation are rich in both imagery and content and leave little doubt in the reader's mind regarding the crisis that is yet to come.

2. Is the Great Tribulation the same as the tribulation?

We believe the Bible distinguishes between the tribulation period (7 years) and the Great Tribulation (the final $3^1/_2$ years).

In Matthew 24:9 the term "tribulation" most likely refers to the full seven-year period of the tribulation. On the other hand, Matthew 24:21 speaks of the "great tribulation," which begins with the abomination of desolation, that takes place at the midpoint of the seven-year period (Matthew 24:15).

In Matthew 24:15-20, Jesus told His disciples that after the midpoint of the tribulation, the Antichrist will break his covenant with Israel. Following this there will be an increase in persecution, "For then there will be a great tribulation, such as has not occurred since the beginning of the world until now, nor ever shall" (Matthew 24:21).

Is the phrase "great tribulation" a technical phrase referring to the last three and a half years of the tribulation, or is it simply a descriptive term for those years? The Bible clearly teaches two segments, but does it label them differently? In other words, does the Bible itself label the first three and a half years as "the tribulation" and the second three and a half years as "the great tribulation," or are the terms "tribulation" and "great tribulation" synonyms for the entire seven-year era?

Premillennial pretribulational interpreters are divided on how this term is used in the Bible. However, *there is no doctrinal orthodoxy or major interpretive issue at stake for whichever view is taken.* For either view, the basic seven-year, two-segment tribulation remains. What changes is how those two segments of three and a half years are labeled. In a formula format, some understand

> seven-year tribulation ($3\frac{1}{2}$ years + $3\frac{1}{2}$ years) = great tribulation ($3\frac{1}{2}$ years + $3\frac{1}{2}$ years)

and others understand

> seven-year tribulation ($3\frac{1}{2}$ years + $3\frac{1}{2}$ years) = tribulation ($3\frac{1}{2}$ years) + great tribulation ($3\frac{1}{2}$ years).

Regardless of the view taken, *both have a seven-year tribulation with two parts and both recognize an increase in intensity during the last three and a half years.*

3. How does "the time of God's wrath" relate to the tribulation?

It appears that "the time of God's wrath" and "the tribulation" encompass the same seven-year time period. How is that so?

Since the Bible uses many terms to describe a wide range of activities associated with God's judgment during the tribulation, and since "tribulation" and "God's wrath" are sometimes used to refer to the same time period (i.e., the seven-year tribulation), then it follows that the time of God's wrath takes place during the tribulation.

Scriptural support can be provided for the above conclusion by the following: We have seen that Deuteronomy 4:30 describes this latter-day time period as a time of tribulation. Zephaniah 1:15 calls this same day "of trouble and distress" (i.e., tribulation) "a day of wrath." New Testament writers pick up this Old Testament term and use it as an overall characteristic of what we know as the seven-year tribulation period, since it is a time when God's stored-up wrath breaks loose within human history and moves to repay a Christ-rejecting world, which will be motivated by Satan to act in persecuting Christians and Jews (Romans 2:5; 5:9; Colossians 3:6; Revelation 14:10, 19; 15:1,7; 16:1,19; 19:15). For example, Romans 2:5 says,

> But because of your stubbornness and unrepentant heart you are storing up wrath for yourself in the day of wrath and revelation of the righteous judgment of God.

Thus we see that what is experienced as tribulation by mankind is said in the Bible to be motivated by the wrath of God, which is shown to be building up during this current age of grace.

4. How do Daniel's 70 weeks relate to the tribulation?

Daniel's 70 weeks, prophesied in Daniel 9:24-27, are the framework within which the tribulation (the seventieth week) occurs.[2] The seven-year period of Daniel's seventieth week provides the time span to which a whole host of descriptives are associated. Some of those descriptive terms include the following: tribulation, great tribulation, day of the Lord, day of wrath, day of distress, day of trouble, time of Jacob's trouble, day of darkness and gloom, wrath of the Lamb, etc. The graphic presentation of the 70 weeks on page 18 assists greatly in understanding this intricate prophecy.

The chart of Daniel's 70 weeks presents a premillennial pretribulational perspective. That is, it shows the rapture occurring before the tribulation and the second coming of Christ

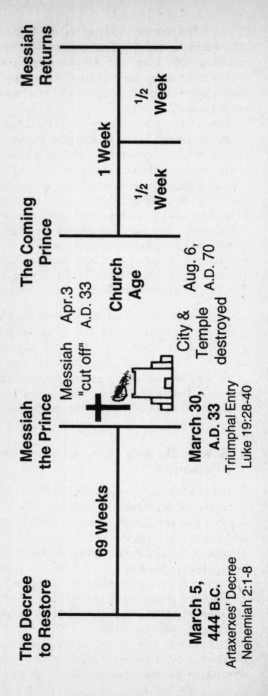

Daniel's Seventy Weeks
(Daniel 9:24-27)

The Decree to Restore

March 5, 444 B.C.
Artaxerxes' Decree
Nehemiah 2:1-8

69 Weeks

Messiah the Prince

March 30, A.D. 33
Triumphal Entry
Luke 19:28-40

Messiah "cut off"

Messiah Apr. 3 A.D. 33

City & Temple destroyed
Aug. 6, A.D. 70

The Coming Prince

Church Age

1 Week

½ Week   ½ Week

Messiah Returns

before the millennium. Although not all evangelicals hold to a pretribulational rapture (favoring instead a midtribulational or post-tribulation view), there is agreement that the Antichrist will arise during the tribulation. He may be known, recognized, or even in power before the rapture, but he will only be revealed or manifested as Antichrist during the tribulation (2 Thessalonians 2:6,8).

Explanation of Daniel's 70 Weeks of Years

$$69 \times 7 \times 360 = 173,880 \text{ days}$$

March 5, 444 B.C. + 173,880 = March 30, A.D. 33

Verification

444 B.C. to A.D. 33 = 476 years

476 years x 365.2421989 days = 173,855 days

+ days between March 5 and March 30 = 25 days

Totals = 173,880 days

Rationale for 360-Day Years

Half week—Daniel 9:27

Time, times, and half a time—Daniel 7:25; 12:7; Revelation 12:14

1260 days—Revelation 12:6; 11:3

42 months—Revelation 11:2; 13:5

Thus: 42 months = 1260 days = time, times, and half a time + half week

Therefore: month = 30 days; year = 360 days[3]

5. How does the "day of the Lord" relate to the tribulation?

The Bible uses the term "day of the Lord" to refer to the same general time period as the tribulation. This was seen earlier in Zephaniah 1:14,15 in which both terms were used to describe different aspects of the same time span.

From God's perspective, this time will be the day of the Lord. It will be a time dominated by and directly under the control of

God. No longer will the Lord control history indirectly through invisible means; during this time He will visibly intervene in human history. Divine intervention then produces, from the human perspective, a time of tribulation to be endured, if possible. Thus, the relationship is that of different perspectives of the same time period.

6. How does "the time of Jacob's trouble" relate to the tribulation?

The phrase "the time of Jacob's trouble" (KJV) or "the time of Jacob's distress" (NASB) comes from the prophecy found in Jeremiah 30:5-7:

> For thus says the LORD, "I have heard a sound of terror, of dread, and there is no peace. Ask now, and see, if a male can give birth. Why do I see every man with his hands on his loins, as a woman in childbirth? And why have all faces turned pale? Alas! for that day is great, there is none like it; and it is the time of Jacob's distress, but he will be saved from it.

In this passage the prophet Jeremiah speaks of a yet-future time when great distress or tribulation will come upon all Israel, which is symbolically referred to as "Jacob." Is this time the same as the coming tribulation, or is it an event already past? It is best to understand this time of distress as something that is yet future for Israel—a time which we know as the seventieth week of Daniel or the tribulation. Biblical expositor and prophecy scholar Dr. Charles H. Dyer writes of this passage and its meaning:

> To what "time of trouble" was Jeremiah referring? Some have felt that he was pointing to the coming fall of Judah to Babylon or to the later fall of Babylon to Medo-Persia. However, in both of these periods the Northern Kingdom of Israel was not affected. It had already gone into captivity (in 722 B.C.). A better solution is to see Jeremiah referring to the still-future Tribulation period when the remnant of Israel and Judah will experience a time of unparalleled persecution (Daniel 9:27; 12:1; Matthew 24:15-22). The period will end when Christ appears to rescue His elect (Romans 11:26) and establish His kingdom (Matthew 24:30-31; 25:31-46; Revelation 19:11-21; 20:4-6).[4]

Thus, the time of Jacob's trouble emphasizes that aspect of the future tribulation which focuses upon the difficulty that Jews or the descendants of Jacob will experience during this time.

7. How does the kingdom of God relate to the tribulation?

While all Bible students generally agree that God always has and will rule spiritually over His creation, this "spiritual" rule is to be distinguished in Scripture from the kingdom of God. Dr. Stanley Toussaint notes that the kingdom of God is "a kingdom that is earthly and literal, and is the fulfillment of the Old Testament promises, covenants, and prophetic predictions for Israel."[5] In other words, the kingdom of God is the future Davidic kingdom, also known as the 1000-year millennium (Revelation 20:2-8).

Having already noted that the tribulation is the seven-year period of our Lord's judgment, then how does it relate to the kingdom of God? The tribulation is the judgment phase which prepares the way for the righteous rule of Christ from Jerusalem. Christ must clean up this sinful world before He commences His 1000-year righteous kingdom.

8. How do "birth pangs" relate to the tribulation?

In Matthew 24:4-7, Jesus describes for the disciples some of the beginning signs of the tribulation. He then states in verse 8, "But all these things are merely the beginning of birth pangs." In the following verses (24:9-28) Jesus continues with a description of the tribulation years. In Jeremiah 30:5-7, the same imagery of childbirth and intense suffering and expectation is used. In these verses God speaks through the prophet:

> For thus says the LORD, "I have heard a sound of terror, of dread, and there is no peace. Ask now, and see, if a male can give birth. Why do I see every man with his hands on his loins, as a woman in childbirth? And why have all faces turned pale? Alas! for that day is great, there is none like it; and it is the time of Jacob's distress, but he will be saved from it."

In this passage, Jeremiah is looking to a time beyond the judgment that was soon to fall on his people. He was referring to

the tribulation era. Dr. Randall Price writes of this passage and
its imagery:

> On the one hand, the figure is applied to the experience
> of tribulation because its application to males or to the
> nation of Israel is tantamount to reducing them to the
> helpless state of women at the time of birth, something
> every army hoped their enemy would become (cf. Jer-
> emiah 50:37). On the other hand, the involuntary and
> uncontrollable nature of birth pangs, as well as their
> intensification leading ultimately to divine deliverance,
> well pictured the concept of a time of divine judgment
> that must run its course until the promise of new life
> could be experienced.[6]

When Jesus spoke of birth pangs in Matthew 24:8, the
imagery used was very clearly that of Jeremiah and other Old
Testament prophets. He is saying that the tribulation will be like
the intense pain of a woman in childbirth. The pain will be great,
but it will end, and with its cessation will come a new era. Note
again the comments of Dr. Price:

> The birth pangs are significant in the timing of the
> Tribulation, as revealed by Jesus in the Olivet discourse
> (Matthew 24:8). Jesus' statement of the "birth pangs" is
> specifically that the events of the first half of the Tribu-
> lation (vv. 4-7) are merely the "beginning," with the
> expectation of greater birth pangs in the second half (the
> "Great Tribulation"). Based on this analogy, the entire
> period of the seventieth week is like birth pangs. As a
> woman must endure the entire period of labor before
> giving birth, so Israel must endure the entire seven-year
> Tribulation. The time divisions of Tribulation are also
> illustrated by the figure, for just as the natural process
> intensifies toward delivery after labor ends, so here the
> Tribulation moves progressively toward the second ad-
> vent (vv. 30-31), which takes place "immediately after"
> the Tribulation ends (v. 29). As there are two phases of
> the birth pangs (beginning labor and full labor), so the
> seven years of Tribulation are divided between the less
> severe and more severe experiences of terrestrial and
> cosmic wrath, as revealed progressively in the Olivet
> discourse and the judgment section of Revelation 6–19.[7]

9. How does the Holy Spirit relate to the tribulation?

When believers are raptured just prior to the tribulation (1 Thessalonians 4:16,17) the indwelling presence of the Holy Spirit will also be removed. We see this in 2 Thessalonians 2:6-8 where Paul writes that once the Holy Spirit as a restrainer is removed from the earth, the "man of lawlessness" (Antichrist) will be free to initiate his program:

> And you know what restrains him now, so that in his time he may be revealed. For the mystery of lawlessness is already at work; only he who now restrains will do so until he is taken out of the way. And then that lawless one will be revealed whom the Lord will slay with the breath of His mouth and bring to an end by the appearance of His coming.

That the Holy Spirit, resident in the church, is the restrainer is supported by the fact that it would take God Himself (in this case, the third Person of the Trinity) to restrain the Antichrist. Dr. Robert Thomas explains:

> To one familiar with the Lord Jesus' Upper Room Discourse, as Paul undoubtedly was, fluctuation between neuter and masculine recalls how the Holy Spirit is spoken of. Either gender is appropriate, depending on whether the speaker (or writer) thinks of natural agreement (masc. because of the Spirit's personality) or grammatical (neuter because of the noun *pneuma*; see John 14:26; 15:26; 16:13,14).... The special presence of the Spirit as the indweller of saints will terminate abruptly at the *parousia* as it began abruptly at Pentecost. Once the body of Christ has been caught away to heaven, the Spirit's ministry will revert back to what he did for believers during the OT period. His function of restraining evil through the body of Christ (John 16:7-11; 1 John 4:4) will cease similarly to the way he terminated his striving in the days of Noah (Genesis 6:3). At that point the reins will be removed from lawlessness and the Satanically inspired rebellion will begin. It appears that *to katechon* ("what is holding back") was well known at Thessalonica as a title for the Holy Spirit on whom the

readers had come to depend in their personal attempts to combat lawlessness (1 Thessalonians 1:6; 4:8; 5:19; 2 Thessalonians 2:13).[8]

The teaching in these verses does not mean, however, that the ministry of the Holy Spirit will be absent during the tribulation. The Holy Spirit will continue to minister, but it will be a much different ministry than Christians experience today. Dr. Ryrie notes, "Just as the omnipresent Spirit worked in behalf of men in Old Testament times, so He will continue to work after the rapture of the Church, even though His work of building the Body of Christ will be finished."[9]

What will be the nature of this ministry and to whom will it be given? In relation to unbelievers, the Spirit will continue to work in bringing about conviction of sin and in the process of salvation. There will be many men and women, Jews and Gentiles, who become Christians during the tribulation, and the Holy Spirit will be active in their salvation (Zechariah 12:10; 13:1; Romans 11:25,26; Revelation 7:9-17). At the beginning of the tribulation, God will seal 144,000 Jewish witnesses, and this sealing entails their salvation and therefore the work of the Spirit (Revelation 7:3,4; 14:4).

According to Acts 2:16-21, which cites Joel 2:28-32 and was partially fulfilled at the day of Pentecost, "EVERYONE WHO CALLS ON THE NAME OF THE LORD WILL BE SAVED." Such a prophetic promise must include the work and ministry of the Holy Spirit. Dr. Walvoord says of this work:

> In view of the natural blindness of the human heart, and the inability of the natural man to understand the gospel sufficiently to believe, apart from the convicting work of the Holy Spirit (John 16:7-11), it must be assumed that there is a continued work of the Holy Spirit in revealing to the lost the way of salvation. This ministry of the Holy Spirit is especially needed in the spiritual darkness which will characterize the tribulation period. We can expect that there will be mighty conviction, especially among Israel, that Christ is indeed the Savior and the Messiah.[10]

Not only will the Holy Spirit be active in relation to unbelievers, but the Spirit will also work in the lives of those who become Christians. While there are few verses from which to discern the complete scope of the Spirit's ministry, it is clear that there will be ministry to believers. There will be preaching of the gospel throughout the world (Matthew 24:14), and many believers will be martyred for their faith. Walvoord notes that "the spiritual victory achieved by the martyrs to the faith in the tribulation could hardly be accomplished apart from the spiritual enablement of the Holy Spirit. The general phenomena of the tribulation make any sort of spiritual achievement unthinkable apart from the power of God."[11]

The ministry to believers will probably be similar to that experienced by some Old Testament saints. Since the Spirit will be removed (2 Thessalonians 2:7), the possibility of a universal indwelling of believers seems unlikely. There will instead be selective indwelling and empowerment to evangelize. Walvoord notes again:

> The tribulation period, also, seems to revert back to Old Testament conditions in several ways; and in the Old Testament period, saints were never permanently indwelt except in isolated instances, though a number of instances of the filling of the Spirit and of empowering for service are found. Taking all the factors into consideration, there is no evidence for the indwelling presence of the Holy Spirit in believers in the tribulation.[12]

PART 2

What Is the Purpose of the Tribulation?

10. Why is the tribulation necessary?

God's basic purpose for the tribulation is that it be a time of judgment, while at the same time holding forth the grace of the gospel, which will precede Christ's glorious 1000-year reign in Jerusalem from David's throne.

Dr. Arnold Fruchtenbaum divides God's purpose into three aspects.[13]

- *To make an end of wickedness and wicked ones.*

    Isaiah 13:9—"Behold, the day of the LORD is coming, cruel, with fury and burning anger, to make the land a desolation; and He will exterminate its sinners from it."

Isaiah 24:19-20—"The earth is broken asunder, the earth is split through, the earth is shaken violently. The earth reels to and fro like a drunkard, and it totters like a shack, for its transgression is heavy upon it, and it will fall, never to rise again."

The first purpose for the tribulation is seen to be a punishment in history upon the whole world for its sins against God, in a way similar to that of the global flood in Noah's time (Matthew 24:37-39).

- *To bring about a worldwide revival.*

  This purpose is given and fulfilled in Revelation 7:1-17: During the first half of the tribulation, God will evangelize the world by the means of the 144,000 Jews and thus fulfill the prophecy found in Matthew 24:14.[14]

  Matthew 24:14—"And this gospel of the kingdom shall be preached in the whole world for a witness to all the nations, and then the end shall come."

- *To break the power of the holy people—Israel.*

  Finally, the tribulation will be a time in which God, through evil agencies, prepares Israel for conversion and acknowledgment that Jesus is her Messiah, resulting in the second coming of Christ. Fruchtenbaum notes:

  > In Daniel 11 and 12, the prophet was given a vision of what conditions will be like for his people (Israel) during the tribulation. Then in Daniel 12:5-7 a question is raised as to how long this period will be allowed to continue.
  >
  > *Daniel 12:5-7*—"Then I, Daniel, looked and behold, two others were standing, one on this bank of the river, and the other on that bank of the river. And one said to the man dressed in linen, who was above the waters of the river, "How long will it be

until the end of these wonders? And I heard the man dressed in linen, who was above the waters of the river, as he raised his right hand and his left toward heaven, and swore by Him who lives forever that it would be for a time, times, and half a time; and as soon as they finish shattering the power of the holy people, all these events will be completed."

This passage provides a third goal of the tribulation. It is to break the power or the stubborn will of the Jewish nation. The tribulation will continue and will not end until this happens. So from this, the third purpose of the tribulation can be deduced: God intends to break the power of the holy people in order to bring about a national regeneration.[15]

11. What are the major events and who are the key personalities of the tribulation?

The seven-year tribulation is divided into two three-and-a-half-year parts. We will look at the major events of each half and events occurring in the middle, knowing that some can be placed in their proper sequence, while other events are harder to place. The chart on page 28 should give a helpful overview.

Events of the First Half of the Tribulation

1. *The seal judgments*—Revelation 6 outlines the seven seal judgments (the seventh contains the trumpet judgments) that kick off the tribulation.[16] The first four seals are also known as the four horsemen of the Apocalypse. These judgments are the beginnings of the wrath of God which is directed at the earth.

2. *The rise of Antichrist and the ten-nation confederacy*— Since the beginning of the tribulation will be marked by the signing of a covenant between Israel and the Antichrist (Daniel 9:26,27), it makes sense that he will come on the scene in the first half of the tribulation. He will be the head of a ten-nation confederacy (Daniel 2:42,44; 7:7,24; Revelation 12:3; 13:1; 17:12,16) that will rule the world during the tribulation.

Seal, Trumpet, and Bowl Judgments

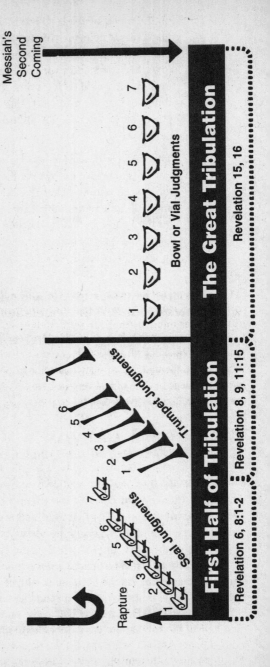

3. *The ministry of Elijah*—Malachi 4:5,6 says,

> Behold, I am going to send you Elijah the prophet before
> the coming of the great and terrible day of the LORD.
> And he will restore the hearts of the fathers to their
> children, and the hearts of the children to their fathers,
> lest I come and smite the land with a curse.

The ministry of Elijah, which could be fulfilled through the
ministry of the two witnesses, will be one of restoration toward
the nation of Israel. Since it will be "before the coming of the
great and terrible day of the LORD," it will occur in the first half
of the tribulation.

4. *The revival through the 144,000 Jewish evangelists*—
Revelation 7 details the call and ministry of 144,000 Jewish
evangelists who preach the gospel during the first half of the
tribulation.

5. *The trumpet judgments*—Revelation 8 and 9 speak of the
trumpet judgments. As with the seal judgments, the seventh
trumpet contains the final series of judgments known as the
bowl judgments. These judgments focus on nature and include
two of the three woe judgments.

6. *The ministry of the two witnesses*—Just as the 144,000 are
engaged in world evangelism, the two witnesses are sealed by
God (Revelation 11:3-6) to be a special witness to Jerusalem and
Israel.

7. *The false church*—Also known as Ecclesiastical Babylon,
it will have great power and influence during the first half of the
tribulation (Revelation 17:1-6). The false church will aid the
Antichrist in his deception.

Events of the
Middle of the Tribulation

1. *The little scroll*—The apostle John is commanded by the
interpreting angel to eat the little book (scroll) in Revelation
10:9-11:

> And I went to the angel, telling him to give me the little
> book. And he said to me, "Take it, and eat it; and it will
> make your stomach bitter, but in your mouth it will be

> sweet as honey." And I took the little book out of the angel's hand and ate it, and it was in my mouth sweet as honey; and when I had eaten it, my stomach was made bitter. And they said to me, "You must prophesy again concerning many peoples and nations and tongues and kings."

The content of the scroll is prophecy relating to the middle and second half of the tribulation. Biblical prophecy is considered good (i.e., sweet) by many people, but the message of judgment (i.e., bitter) is hard to take.

2. *The Antichrist is killed*—Revelation 13:3 notes that the seventh head (a reference to the Antichrist) is killed. As we will note later, he is not yet finished.

> And I saw one of his heads as if it had been slain, and his fatal wound was healed. And the whole earth was amazed and followed after the beast.

3. *Satan cast down to the earth from heaven*—Revelation 12:7-9 reveals that Satan himself is cast to the earth from heaven through angelic agency. This provides the basis for an intensification of events upon earth during the second half of the tribulation:

> And there was war in heaven, Michael and his angels waging war with the dragon. And the dragon and his angels waged war, and they were not strong enough, and there was no longer a place found for them in heaven. And the great dragon was thrown down, the serpent of old who is called the devil and Satan, who deceives the whole world; he was thrown down to the earth, and his angels were thrown down with him.

4. *The resurrection of the Antichrist*—One of the first things Satan does on earth after being cast out of heaven is to resurrect the Antichrist. Revelation 13:3,4 records this episode as the Antichrist attempts to counterfeit the career of Jesus, the Messiah:

And I saw one of his heads as if it had been slain, and his fatal wound was healed. And the whole earth was amazed and followed after the beast; and they worshiped the dragon, because he gave his authority to the beast; and they worshiped the beast, saying, "Who is like the beast, and who is able to wage war with him?"

5. *Three kings killed and seven submit*—After his death and resurrection, Antichrist consolidates his worldwide rule by killing three of the ten kings, which leads to the other seven submitting voluntarily. This event provides the political basis from which Antichrist will project his power during the last half of the tribulation:

> As for the ten horns, out of this kingdom ten kings will arise; and another will arise after them, and he will be different from the previous ones and will subdue three kings (Daniel 7:24).

> And the ten horns which you saw are ten kings, who have not yet received a kingdom, but they receive authority as kings with the beast for one hour. These have one purpose and they give their power and authority to the beast (Revelation 17:12,13).

6. *Destruction of the false church*—As has often been the case historically, when a tyrant reaches his goal of total political control, he destroys those who helped him reach that point. Antichrist now destroys the harlot, Ecclesiastical Babylon, as noted in Revelation 17:16:

> And the ten horns which you saw, and the beast, these will hate the harlot and will make her desolate and naked, and will eat her flesh and will burn her up with fire.

7. *The death and resurrection of the two witnesses*—God enables the temporary deception of Antichrist to proceed further with the death of the two witnesses. During the first half of the tribulation, the two witnesses were miraculously protected by God. God now allows the deception of Antichrist to deepen

when he murders the two witnesses in Jerusalem, and the whole world rejoices. However, after three and a half days the two witnesses will be resurrected and taken to heaven in the sight of all. Fear then grips those who have followed after the beast:

> And when they have finished their testimony, the beast that comes up out of the abyss will make war with them, and overcome them and kill them. And their dead bodies will lie in the street of the great city which mystically is called Sodom and Egypt, where also their Lord was crucified. And those from the peoples and tribes and tongues and nations will look at their dead bodies for three and a half days, and will not permit their dead bodies to be laid in a tomb. And those who dwell on the earth will rejoice over them and make merry; and they will send gifts to one another, because these two prophets tormented those who dwell on the earth. And after the three and a half days the breath of life from God came into them, and they stood on their feet; and great fear fell upon those who were beholding them. And they heard a loud voice from heaven saying to them, "Come up here." And they went up into heaven in the cloud, and their enemies beheld them. And in that hour there was a great earthquake, and a tenth of the city fell; and seven thousand people were killed in the earthquake, and the rest were terrified and gave glory to the God of heaven (Revelation 11:7-13).

8. *The worship of the Antichrist*—Since the "earth dwellers" prefer the counterfeit over the genuine, they will be deceived into worshiping the Antichrist as God. In reality, they will be worshiping Satan. No wonder the Bible is filled with warnings about spiritual deception!

> And I saw one of his heads as if it had been slain, and his fatal wound was healed. And the whole earth was amazed and followed after the beast; and they worshiped the dragon, because he gave his authority to the beast; and they worshiped the beast, saying, "Who is like the beast, and who is able to wage war with him?" (Revelation 13:3,4).

> And all who dwell on the earth will worship him, everyone whose name has not been written from the foundation of the world in the book of life of the Lamb who has been slain (Revelation 13:8).

9. *The false prophet*—This person is a counterfeit of the ministry of the Holy Spirit in that he is temporarily empowered to do false signs, wonders, and miracles which greatly aid the Antichrist's rise to power. False religion is the vehicle of deception for this second beast—the false prophet:

> And I saw another beast coming up out of the earth; and he had two horns like a lamb, and he spoke as a dragon. And he exercises all the authority of the first beast in his presence. And he makes the earth and those who dwell in it to worship the first beast, whose fatal wound was healed. And he performs great signs, so that he even makes fire come down out of heaven to the earth in the presence of men. And he deceives those who dwell on the earth because of the signs which it was given him to perform in the presence of the beast, telling those who dwell on the earth to make an image to the beast who had the wound of the sword and has come to life. And there was given to him to give breath to the image of the beast, that the image of the beast might even speak and cause as many as do not worship the image of the beast to be killed (Revelation 13:11-15).

10. *666—The mark of the beast*—Another "ministry" of the false prophet will be the administering of the counterfeit seal of the Holy Spirit: the famous mark of the beast, 666. Placement of this mark on the forehead or right hand will be required to conduct economic transactions during the second half of the tribulation. It should be noted that any person receiving this mark cannot be saved. This mark will not be distributed during the first half of the tribulation, but only during the latter half. Since the meaning of 666 is a mystery, it is not wise to speculate about this until the time in which it is distributed. It is clear that its meaning will be evident to believers during the tribulation:

> And he causes all, the small and the great, and the rich and the poor, and the free men and the slaves, to be

given a mark on their right hand, or on their forehead, and he provides that no one should be able to buy or to sell, except the one who has the mark, either the name of the beast or the number of his name. Here is wisdom. Let him who has understanding calculate the number of the beast, for the number is that of a man; and his number is six hundred and sixty-six (Revelation 13:16-18).

11. *The seven-year covenant broken*—It is not at all surprising that the Antichrist should break his covenant with Israel. Such a move is in keeping with his character. This betrayal will involve Antichrist's military invasion of Israel:

He will also enter the Beautiful Land, and many countries will fall; but these will be rescued out of his hand: Edom, Moab and the foremost of the sons of Ammon (Daniel 11:41).

And your covenant with death shall be canceled, and your pact with Sheol shall not stand; when the overwhelming scourge passes through, then you become its trampling place (Isaiah 28:18).

12. *The abomination of desolation*—Antichrist will not only break his covenant with Israel, but he will also set himself up as God to be worshiped in the rebuilt Jewish temple at the midpoint of the tribulation. This defiling of the third temple is called "the abomination of desolation." This will be a sign to the Jews to flee Jerusalem:

And he will make a firm covenant with the many for one week, but in the middle of the week he will put a stop to sacrifice and grain offering; and on the wing of abominations will come one who makes desolate, even until a complete destruction, one that is decreed, is poured out on the one who makes desolate (Daniel 9:27).

Therefore when you see the ABOMINATION OF DESOLATION which was spoken of through Daniel the prophet, standing in the holy place (let the reader understand), then let those who are in Judea flee to the mountains (Matthew 24:15,16).

...who opposes and exalts himself above every so-called god or object of worship, so that he takes his seat in the temple of God, displaying himself as being God (2 Thessalonians 2:4).

13. *The persecution of the Jews*—The second half of the tribulation will be characterized by an extreme attempt to wipe the Jews off the face of the earth. Likely, Satan's thinking on this matter is that if the Jews are exterminated, then God's plan for history will have been thwarted. Satan might think that this would somehow prevent the second coming. This persecution is pictured in Revelation 12:1-6. Within the imagery, the woman represents Israel, and her male child represents Christ:

> And a great sign appeared in heaven: a woman clothed with the sun, and the moon under her feet, and on her head a crown of twelve stars; and she was with child; and she cried out, being in labor and in pain to give birth. And another sign appeared in heaven: and behold, a great red dragon having seven heads and ten horns, and on his heads were seven diadems. And his tail swept away a third of the stars of heaven, and threw them to the earth. And the dragon stood before the woman who was about to give birth, so that when she gave birth he might devour her child. And she gave birth to a son, a male child, who is to rule all the nations with a rod of iron; and her child was caught up to God and to His throne. And the woman fled into the wilderness where she had a place prepared by God, so that there she might be nourished for one thousand two hundred and sixty days.

Events of the Second Half of the Tribulation

1. *The bowl judgments*—The bowl judgments are the most severe series of judgments of the whole tribulation. They occur in the second half of the tribulation, devastate Antichrist's kingdom, and prepare the way for the second coming of Christ. The bowl judgments are the result of the prayers of the saints for God to take revenge on their behalf (Revelation 15:1-8). The bowl judgments are described in Revelation 16.

2. *The protection of the Jewish remnant*—At the midpoint of the tribulation the Jews will flee when the Antichrist commits the abomination of desolation. Apparently these Jews will be protected in the Jordanian village of Bozrah, known also as Petra. A remnant will be preserved through this and other means:

> I will surely assemble all of you, Jacob, I will surely gather the remnant of Israel. I will put them together like sheep in the fold [literally, Bozrah]; like a flock in the midst of its pasture they will be noisy with men (Micah 2:12).

> Then let those who are in Judea flee to the mountains (Matthew 24:16).

> And the woman fled into the wilderness where she had a place prepared by God, so that there she might be nourished for one thousand two hundred and sixty days (Revelation 12:6).

> And the two wings of the great eagle were given to the woman, in order that she might fly into the wilderness to her place, where she was nourished for a time and times and half a time, from the presence of the serpent (Revelation 12:14).

3. *The conversion of Israel*—Right before the second coming, Israel will be converted to the Messiahship of Jesus and saved from their sins. This will prepare them for their role in the millennial kingdom after the second advent:

> And I will pour out on the house of David and on the inhabitants of Jerusalem, the Spirit of grace and of supplication, so that they will look on Me whom they have pierced; and they will mourn for Him, as one mourns for an only son, and they will weep bitterly over Him, like the bitter weeping over a first-born. (Zechariah 12:10).

> For I do not want you, brethren, to be uninformed of this mystery, lest you be wise in your own estimation, that a partial hardening has happened to Israel until the fulness of the Gentiles has come in; and thus all Israel will be saved; just as it is written, "THE DELIVERER WILL COME FROM ZION, HE WILL REMOVE UNGODLINESS FROM JACOB. AND THIS IS MY COVENANT WITH THEM, WHEN I TAKE AWAY THEIR SINS" (Romans 11:25-27).

P A R T 3

When Will
the Tribulation Occur?

12. Has the tribulation occurred in the past?

On the night He was betrayed, Jesus told His disciples, "In the world you have tribulation, but take courage; I have overcome the world" (John 16:33). With these words, Jesus stated that tribulation or hardship would be a continual reality in the lives of those who followed Him throughout the current church age. Christian martyrs throughout the history of the church have certainly proven the veracity of His words.

However, the tribulation of Daniel's seventieth week is a completely different era. The tribulation of God's prophetic plan is much greater and of a different purpose than that of which Jesus spoke in John 16. The tribulation of the future is not the same as the daily trials and struggles of Christians throughout church history. This is not to belittle the pain, hardship, suffering, and even death that those who follow Christ have often endured. Rather, it is to say that the future will bring even greater and more widespread trials which will culminate in the seventieth week. Also, current trials and tribulation are directed against us today by the world (John 15:18-25) as a hardship for following Christ. The tribulation is a time of God's wrath which will come upon the people of the earth to test them (Revelation 3:10; 6:15-17).

Some interpreters of prophecy wish to argue that the tribulation is already past. This view is called "preterism" (Latin for "past") and holds that all prophecies relating to the tribulation are now history and were fulfilled during the first century A.D., usually revolving around events associated with the destruction of Jerusalem in A.D. 70.

Preterism cannot be supported from Scripture for at least two major reasons. First, in order to support the notion of an A.D. 70 fulfillment of the large number of details surrounding the tribulation, preterists must use an unwarranted allegorical interpretative approach. This means that passages such as Matthew 24:30 and Revelation 19:11-21, which have traditionally been interpreted as references to Christ's second coming, must somehow be understood to really represent Christ coming mysteriously through the Roman army which conquered Jerusalem in A.D. 70. Such an approach exceeds the legitimate hermeneutical disagreements over figurative versus normal use of figures of speech and commits the error of spiritualization by supplying a meaning not supported by textual interpretation.

A second major error of preterism is the confusion of judgment and salvation in relation to the nation of Israel. Preterism sees only judgment toward Israel in passages that speak of the tribulation, such as the Olivet discourse (Matthew 24; Mark 13; Luke 17:20-37; 21:5-36) and Revelation 4–19. Except for Luke 21:20-24, which clearly speaks of the A.D. 70 judgment upon Jerusalem, the rest of the passages picture Israel in a position from which God will deliver them from their enemies through His second coming. Even their allegorical approach to the biblical text cannot hide the clear fact that tribulation passages describe our Lord's salvation of Israel, not His judgment upon them.[17]

13. Are we currently in the tribulation?

Even though believers during the current church age experience trials and tribulation (John 15:18-25; 16:33; 2 Timothy 2:12), these are not the trials of the tribulation, from which the church has been promised removal (Revelation 3:10). Thus, we are not currently in the tribulation.

14. Will the tribulation take place in the future?

According to the prophetic timeline of Daniel 9:24-27 and 2 Thessalonians 2, the tribulation will follow the rapture of the church. This event, which is yet future, will terminate the present interval between the sixty-ninth and seventieth weeks of Daniel and will allow the tribulation to begin. Dr. Ryrie writes of this era:

> The Tribulation does not necessarily begin the day the church is taken to meet the Lord in the air. Though I believe that the Rapture precedes the beginning of the Tribulation, actually nothing is said in the Scriptures as to whether or not some time (or how much time) may elapse between the Rapture and the beginning of the Tribulation.
>
> The Tribulation actually begins with the signing of a covenant between the leader of the "Federated States of

Europe" and the Jewish people. This treaty will set in motion the events of the seventieth week (or seven years) of Daniel's prophecy. There is an interval of undetermined length between the first sixty-nine weeks of seven years each and the last or seventieth week of seven years.[18]

Since none of the events of the tribulation have yet taken place (Antichrist's signing a covenant with Israel, the revelation of the Antichrist, the abomination of desolation, the mark of the beast, etc.), then it stands to reason that the tribulation is yet future.

P A R T   4

How Long Is the Tribulation?

15. Where does the Bible teach a seven-year tribulation?

Belief that the tribulation will last for seven years comes from the prophetic calendar of Daniel 9:24-27, specifically from verse 27:

> And he [the Antichrist] will make a firm covenant with the many for one week, but in the middle of the week he will put a stop to sacrifice and grain offering; and on the wing of abominations will come one who makes desolate, even until a complete destruction, one that is decreed, is poured out on the one who makes desolate.

The "week" that Daniel writes of is understood by most prophecy scholars to be a "week of years" or seven years. These years follow the interval of the "seven weeks and sixty-two weeks" found in Daniel 9:25. In Daniel 9:2, Daniel was thinking about the years of Israel's captivity by the Babylonians. This captivity had been prophesied by Jeremiah as being a period of 70 years:

> "This whole land shall be a desolation and a horror, and these nations shall serve the king of Babylon seventy

years. Then it will be when seventy years are completed I will punish the king of Babylon and that nation," declares the LORD, "for their iniquity, and the land of the Chaldeans; and I will make it an everlasting desolation" (Jeremiah 25:11,12).

For thus says the LORD, "When seventy years have been completed for Babylon, I will visit you and fulfill My good word to you, to bring you back to this place" (Jeremiah 29:10).

As Daniel studied the words of Jeremiah and prayed (Daniel 9:3-19), the angel Gabriel appeared to him revealing the prophetic timetable found in Daniel 9:24-27. The Hebrew term used for "weeks" in this passage means "sevens" or "units of seven," without specifying whether it means days, months, or years. In this passage only "years" fits the timetable since a period of 490 days or 490 months is historically too short a time span. The 70 weeks must be a period of 490 years (70 x 7). The seventieth week must also therefore be a period of seven years. Dr. Walvoord writes of this:

The only system of interpretation, however, that gives any literal meaning to this prophecy is to regard the time units as prophetic years of 360 days each according to the Jewish custom of having years of 360 days with an occasional extra month inserted to correct the calendar as needed. The seventy times seven is, therefore, 490 years with the beginning at the time of "the commandment to restore and rebuild Jerusalem" found in verse 25 and the culmination of 490 years later in verse 27. Before detailing the events between the sixty-ninth seven and the seventieth seven, and the final seven years, Daniel gives the overall picture in verse 24. Careful attention must be given to the precise character of this important foundational prophecy.[19]

16. How do the time indicators of Revelation fit into the tribulation?

The book of Revelation gives a number of time indicators. These include:

- time, times, and half a time (i.e., 3½ years) (Revelation 12:14)

- 1260 days (Revelation 11:3)
- 42 months (Revelation 11:2; 13:5)

These time indicators, each a different way of indicating three and a half years, reflect the two halves of the seven-year tribulation period of the seventieth week as developed from Daniel 9:24-27.

17. Is the Great Tribulation of different length than the tribulation?

Since we have noted in question 2 that the tribulation refers to the entire seven years of Daniel's seventieth week, while the Great Tribulation is the second half of that seven-year period, it would follow that they are thus different lengths.

P A R T   5

Who Will Be in the Tribulation?

18. How does Israel relate to the tribulation?

In question 10, we saw that one of the major reasons for the tribulation was to prepare Israel for her conversion. Thus, both Israel as a nation and a people will experience the manifestations of evil during this era. In fact, many of the events of the tribulation revolve around Israel. Both geographically and spiritually, Israel is at center stage during the tribulation.

19. How do the Gentiles relate to the tribulation?

Because the tribulation is worldwide in its scope, all people or nations will be affected. As during the flood of Noah's time, there will be no escape. Thus, the Gentiles will be judged for their treatment of Israel and their rejection of Jesus as the Lord and Savior of humanity. However, multitudes of Gentiles will come to faith in Christ during the tribulation:

> After these things I looked, and behold, a great multitude, which no one could count, from every nation and

all tribes and peoples and tongues, standing before the
throne and before the Lamb, clothed in white robes, and
palm branches were in their hands; and they cry out with
a loud voice, saying, "Salvation to our God who sits on
the throne, and to the Lamb" (Revelation 7:9,10).

20. How does the church relate to the tribulation?

Prior to the beginning of the tribulation, Jesus Christ will
appear in the clouds and both dead and living believers will be
raptured or "caught up" to Him. The central passage for this is
found in 1 Thessalonians 4:16,17:

For the Lord Himself will descend from heaven with a
shout, with the voice of the archangel, and with the
trumpet of God; and the dead in Christ shall rise first.
Then we who are alive and remain shall be caught up
together with them in the clouds to meet the Lord in the
air, and so we shall always be with the Lord.

When the rapture occurs, the church as we know it today will
be gathered to the Lord and therefore will not be present on earth
during the tribulation. This is confirmed by Paul in 1 Thessalonians and John in Revelation. Paul encourages Christians to
"wait for His Son from heaven, whom He raised from the dead,
that is Jesus, who rescues us from the wrath to come" (1 Thessalonians 1:10). Paul continues in 1 Thessalonians 5:1-11 to describe the tribulation era and related events. He assures his
readers that the church will not endure this time, "For God has
not destined us for wrath, but for obtaining salvation through our
Lord Jesus Christ, who died for us, that whether we are awake or
asleep, we may live together with Him" (1 Thessalonians
5:9,10).

Dr. Walvoord summarizes this passage very clearly:

This is a categorical denial that the church will go
through the tribulation which is described as a day of
wrath (Revelation 6:17). The whole argument of this
section is that the Christian will not enter the Day of the
Lord, that he belongs to a different day, that he is
looking for the coming of the Lord and not the Day of
the Lord. The idea sometimes advanced that the Christian will be preserved through the tribulation and in this

sense will be kept from the wrath of God is beside the point. It is not that the Christian will be kept from wrath which, of course, is always true under all circumstances even if a Christian is martyred; but it is rather that this is not our appointment. The characteristics of the day of wrath, unfolded in the book of Revelation and antici- pated in prophecies concerning the Day of the Lord in the Old Testament, reveal forms of divine judgment which inevitably will afflict the entire human race. War, pestilence, famine, earthquakes, and stars falling from heaven are not by their nature selective but are almost universal in their application. This is not the Christian's appointment who is looking for the coming of the Lord at the rapture.[20]

This preservation from the tribulation or "wrath to come" is reiterated by John who records the Lord's words, "Because you have kept the word of My perseverance, I also will keep you from the hour of testing, that hour which is about to come upon the whole world, to test those who dwell upon the earth" (Revelation 3:10).

The church as the body of Christ will not be present during the tribulation. Dr. Walvoord writes:

The nature of the tribulation, if Scriptures relating to it are interpreted normally and literally, gives no basis for the idea that the church, the body of Christ, the saints of this present age, will be forced to remain on earth through it. According to the Scriptures, it is specifically the time of Jacob's trouble (Jeremiah 30:7) and coin- cides with the last seven years of Israel's program as outlined in Daniel 9:24-27.... The fact is most signifi- cant that the terms normally used of the church and which set it apart as distinct from saints of previous ages are never found in any tribulation passage.... That there is reference to Israel, to saints, to saved Israelites, and to saved Gentiles does not prove that the church is in this period as these terms are general terms, not spe- cific.[21]

Although the church is not present during the tribulation, there will be men and women who come to a saving knowledge of Jesus Christ. There will be redeemed individuals living on earth during the tribulation. Dr. Walvoord notes:

> The elect or the saved of the tribulation period are composed of both Jews and Gentiles who turn to Christ for salvation. During the early part of the period between the rapture and the second coming of Christ, there is some religious freedom as indicated by the restoration of Jewish sacrifices. With the beginning of the great tribulation, however, this freedom is abruptly ended, and Jewish sacrifices cease. All who oppose the deification and worship of the world dictator are subject to persecution. Both Jew and Christian become the objects of this satanic oppression, and many are martyred. The elect are delivered by the return of Christ at the close of the tribulation period.[22]

We read in Revelation 6:9-11:

> And when He broke the fifth seal, I saw underneath the altar the souls of those who had been slain because of the word of God, and because of the testimony which they had maintained; and they cried out with a loud voice, saying, "How long, O Lord, holy and true, wilt Thou refrain from judging and avenging our blood on those who dwell on the earth?" And there was given to each of them a white robe; and they were told that they should rest for a little while longer, until the number of their fellow servants and their brethren who were to be killed even as they had been, should be completed also.

These verses describe the fifth seal judgment and presuppose prior events happening on earth. The fact that verse 9 speaks of martyrs implies that they are believers who were killed early in the tribulation because of their faith.

There is also the witness of the 144,000 Jews described in Revelation 7:1-8. Dr. Ryrie writes of these people:

> They are Jews from each of the twelve tribes, and they do some particular service for God. Whether the seal placed on them [Revelation 7:3] is a visible mark or characteristic of some kind is neither stated nor implied

in the text. A seal need not be visible to be real (Ephesians 4:30). It is principally a guarantee of ownership and security. Both these ideas are involved in the sealing of this group. These people are owned by God, which means that they are redeemed. They are kept secure by God, which may mean He protects them from their enemies on earth while they complete their service for Him.[23]

Following the rapture there will still be Bibles, religious literature, and many people who knew the gospel before the rapture but had not yet converted to Christianity. These materials will be used, and many previously evangelized unbelievers will come to faith in Jesus Christ. It is through these means and these people, in addition to the ministry of the 144,000, that there will be Christians during the tribulation. We read in Revelation 14:4 that the 144,000 "have been purchased from among men as first fruits to God and to the Lamb." This is further confirmation that there will be many new believers during this time. And just as in the early days of the faith, many will be martyred because of their beliefs.

P A R T   6

Why Does the Tribulation Matter?

21. Why should I be concerned about the tribulation?

The tribulation is important for Christians today for several reasons. First, the study of God's Word is always important, and it is to be handled with great care. Regardless of the type of passages studied, whether covenant or chronology, poetry, parable, or prophecy, all are to be diligently studied and applied. "All Scripture is inspired by God and profitable for teaching, for reproof, for correction, for training in righteousness; that the man of God may be adequate, equipped for every good work" (2 Timothy 3:16,17). The tribulation is important because Scripture teaches it.

Second, the tribulation is important because, in a sense, Satan is unmasked and we see his ultimate intentions and purposes. Such an understanding of his plan, if properly applied, can aid the believer today in spiritual warfare.

For example, we note that during the tribulation, Satan uses religion in a false and deceptive way. This stands as a warning for us today.

Third, the tribulation is important to us because much of what we see today and have seen in the past is a forerunner of that which will come. For example, the current impulse toward globalism should not be surprising for those who are aware of what the Bible teaches is yet ahead. Because our Sovereign God has foreordained such events, we should take comfort from the fact that He is in control. This future time of evil is the full development of humanity's sinful nature in conjunction with Satan's rebellious plan. Yet both will be brought under the judgment of a righteous and omnipotent God.

Conclusion

Human history has been filled with personal, national, and international tragedy and despair. In every century, every empire, and every era there have been multiple manifestations of original sin, the Fall, and satanic activity. Passages of biblical prophecy (and other portions of Scripture) clearly teach that the future will bring a specific period of increased trauma and tragedy during which terror and tribulation will be both intense and international. This era will last for seven years and, following the battle of Armageddon, will culminate in the second coming of the Lord Jesus Christ to establish His millennial kingdom and reign on earth. We believe that this tribulation era of destruction and persecution will follow the rapture of the church. However, such a belief does not alleviate contemporary Christians of daily responsibilities, evangelism, discipleship, or holy living. Tribulation is certain, but so is triumph. Concerning the tribulation, it is not the living of *those* days about which we need to be concerned; rather, it is the living of *these* days. "Therefore be careful how you walk, not as unwise men but as wise, making the most of your time, because the days are evil" (Ephesians 5:16,17).

Notes

1. For a more thorough treatment of these passages, see J. Randall Price, "Old Testament Tribulation Terms," in *When the Trumpet Sounds*, eds. Thomas Ice and Timothy Demy (Eugene, OR: Harvest House Publishers, 1995), pp. 57-84.

2. One of the most readable and extensive discussions on the chronology of the 70 weeks is found in Harold W. Hoehner, *Chronological Aspects of the Life of Christ* (Grand Rapids: Zondervan Publishing House, 1977), pp. 115-39. A more popular presentation is Herb Vander Lugt, *The Daniel Papers* (Grand Rapids: Radio Bible Class, 1994).

3. Hoehner, *Chronological*, p. 139.

4. Charles H. Dyer, "Jeremiah" in *The Bible Knowledge Commentary: Old Testament*, eds. John F. Walvoord and Roy B. Zuck (Wheaton, IL: Victor Books, 1984), p. 1168.

5. Stanley D. Toussaint, "The Contingency of the Coming of the Kingdom" in *Integrity of Heart, Skillfulness of Hands: Biblical and Leadership Studies in Honor of Donald K. Campbell*, eds. Charles H. Dyer and Roy B. Zuck (Grand Rapids: Baker Book House, 1994), p. 224.

6. Price, "Old Testament Tribulation Terms," p. 71.

7. Ibid., p. 72.

8. "2 Thessalonians," *The Expositor's Bible Commentary*, 12 vols., Robert L. Thomas, Frank Gaebelein, general editors (Grand Rapids: Zondervan, 1978), 11:224-25.

9. Charles C. Ryrie, *The Holy Spirit* (Chicago: Moody Press, 1965), p. 108.

10. John F. Walvoord, *The Holy Spirit* (Findlay, OH: Dunham Publishing Co., 1958), p. 229.

11. Ibid., p. 231.

12. Ibid., p. 230.

13. Arnold G. Fruchtenbaum, *The Footsteps of the Messiah: A Study of the Sequence of Prophetic Events* (San Antonio: Ariel Press, 1982), pp. 122-26.

14. Ibid., pp. 123-24.

15. Ibid., p. 125.

16. We are following events as outlined in Fruchtenbaum, *Footsteps,* pp. 135-91.

17. For more extensive interaction with preterism see H. Wayne House and Thomas Ice, *Dominion Theology: Blessing or Curse? An Analysis of Christian Reconstructionism* (Portland: Multnomah Press, 1988), pp. 249-334.

18. Charles C. Ryrie, *Basic Theology* (Wheaton, IL: Victor Books, 1986), p. 465.

19. John F. Walvoord, *Daniel: The Key to Prophetic Revelation* (Chicago: Moody Press, 1971), pp. 219-20.

20. John F. Walvoord, *The Church in Prophecy* (Grand Rapids: Zondervan Publishing House, 1964), p. 91.

21. Ibid., pp. 129-30.

22. John F. Walvoord, *The Millennial Kingdom* (Findlay, OH: Dunham Publishing Co., 1958), pp. 257-58.

23. Ryrie, *Basic Theology*, p. 468.

Recommended Reading

Dyer, Charles H. *World News and Bible Prophecy*. Wheaton, IL: Tyndale House Publishers, 1993.

Fruchtenbaum, Arnold. *The Footsteps of the Messiah: A Study of the Sequence of Prophetic Events*. San Antonio, TX: Ariel Press, 1982.

Hoehner, Harold W. *Chronological Aspects of the Life of Christ*. Grand Rapids: Zondervan Publishing House, 1977.

Hunt, Dave. *A Cup of Trembling: Jerusalem and Bible Prophecy*. Eugene, OR: Harvest House Publishers, 1995.

Ice, Thomas and Demy, Timothy, eds. *When the Trumpet Sounds: Today's Foremost Authorities Speak Out on End-Time Controversies*. Eugene, OR: Harvest House Publishers, 1995.

Ice, Thomas and Price, Randall. *Ready to Rebuild: The Imminent Plan to Rebuild the Last Days Temple*. Eugene, OR: Harvest House Publishers, 1992.

Lindsey, Hal. *The Late Great Planet Earth*. Grand Rapids: Zondervan Publishing House, 1970.

Pentecost, J. Dwight. *Things to Come: A Study in Biblical Eschatology*. Grand Rapids: Zondervan Publishing House, 1958.

Thomas, Robert L. *Revelation: An Exegetical Commentary*. 2 vols. Chicago: Moody Press, 1992, 1995.

Walvoord, John F. *Daniel: The Key to Prophetic Revelation*. Chicago: Moody Press, 1971.

_____. *Major Bible Prophecies: 37 Crucial Prophecies That Affect You Today*. Grand Rapids: Zondervan Publishing House, 1991.

_____. *Prophecy: 14 Essential Keys to Understanding the Final Drama*. Nashville: Thomas Nelson Publishers, 1993.

_____. *The Prophecy Knowledge Handbook*. Wheaton, IL: SP Publications, 1990.

_____. *Israel in Prophecy*. Grand Rapids: Zondervan Publishing House, 1962.

_____. *The Nations in Prophecy*. Grand Rapids: Zondervan Publishing House, 1967.

_____. *The Revelation of Jesus Christ*. Chicago: Moody Press, 1963.